# · *Cooking for Today* ·

# COOKING ON A BUDGET

·*Cooking for Today*·

# COOKING ON A BUDGET

SUE ASHWORTH

SMITHMARK

Distributed in the USA by SMITHMARK Publishers,
a division of U.S. Media Holdings Inc.,
16, East 32nd Street, New York, NY 10016

SMITHMARK books are available for bulk purchase for sales promotion and premium use.
For details, write or call the Manager of Special Sales, SMITHMARK publishers,
16 East 32nd Street, New York, NY 10016; (212) 532-6600

ISBN: 0 - 7651 - 9850 - 9

10 9 8 7 6 5 4 3 2 1

Printed in Italy

**Acknowledgements:**
*Art Direction:* Ron Samuels
*Editor:* Vicky Hanson
*Series Design:* Pedro & Frances Prá-Lopez/Kingfisher Design, London
*Page Design:* Somewhere Creative
*Photography & Styling:* Amanda Heywood
*Home Economist:* Sue Ashworth
*Assistant Home Economist:* Yvonne Melville

Photographs on pages 6, 20, 34, 48 & 62 reproduced by permission of
ZEFA Picture Library (UK) Ltd.

*Note:*
*Cup measurements in this book are for American cups. Tablespoons are assumed to be 15 ml.*
*Unless otherwise stated, milk is assumed to be full-fat, eggs are standard size 2 and*
*pepper is freshly ground black pepper.*

# Contents

**SOUPS & STEWS** *page 7*

Cream Cheese & Fresh Herb Soup .......................8
Lentil & Parsnip Potage .........................10
Lamb & Barley Broth ..........................12
Italian Fish Stew ...........................15
Chicken & Chili Bean Pot .......................16
Beef Goulash ...........................18

**PIES & BAKES** *page 21*

Baked Stuffed Onions ..........................22
Winter Vegetable Cobbler .........................24
Mariner's Pie ...........................26
Ground Lamb & Potato Moussaka ......................29
Savory Batter Popovers with Thyme &
   Onion Sauce ...........................30
Bacon, Onion, & Potato Hotpot .......................32

**PASTA, RICE, & GRAINS** *page 35*

Thai-Style Chicken-Fried Rice ............................36
Mushroom & Parmesan Risotto .........................38
Pasta with Pine Kernels & Blue Cheese ...............41
Smoked Fish Lasagne ...........................42
Quick Chinese Chicken with Noodles .................44
Moroccan Vegetable Couscous ...........................46

**EGGS & CHEESE** *page 49*

Egg & Garbanzo Bean Curry ...................................50
Savory Bread & Butter Bake ...........................52
Spinach & Cheese Pancake Stack .......................55
Chicken & Corn Puff ...........................56
Golden Cheese & Leek Potato Patties .................58
Flamenco Eggs ...........................60

**DESSERTS** *page 63*

Chocolate Bread Pudding ...........................64
Quick Syrup Sponge ...........................66
Pancakes with Apples & Butterscotch Sauce .......68
Apricot & Banana Queen of Puddings .................70
Baked Semolina Pudding with Spiced Plums .......73
Coffee Cream Trifle ...........................74

**KEEPING TO A BUDGET** *page 76*

Index ...................................80

# CHAPTER ONE

# *Soups & Stews*

Tasty, filling, and nutritious, soups and stews are the original comfort food. Perfect for when you are feeling cold and hungry, these recipes will satisfy your appetite and fill you to the brim – even when you're having to feed everyone on a budget.

The trick is to make the most of fresh seasonal vegetables, and to treat them with flair and a pinch of imagination. Some of the cheapest ingredients are transformed into something special in the recipes in this chapter. Who would have thought that a few handfuls of fresh herbs from the garden could be transformed into the most delicious summer soup (see page 8)? And who wouldn't enjoy the aromas from the slow-cooked Lamb & Barley Broth (see page 12) as it bubbles away on the stove?

So try these ideas and introduce some superb new recipes into your repertoire – you'll be delighted with the results. What's more, you'll find that your family budget won't be overstretched.

Opposite: *Use ingredients that are in season and you'll find that soups and stews are so economical.*

STEP 1

STEP 2

STEP 3

STEP 4

# CREAM CHEESE & FRESH HERB SOUP

*Make the most of homegrown herbs to create this wonderfully creamy soup with its marvelous summer-fresh fragrance.*

SERVES 4

2 tbsp butter or margarine
2 onions, chopped
3¹/₂ cups vegetable stock
1 oz coarsely chopped mixed fresh herbs,
    such as parsley, chives, thyme, basil, and
    oregano
1 cup full-fat soft cheese
1 tbsp cornstarch
1 tbsp milk
chopped fresh chives to garnish

**1** Melt the butter or margarine in a large saucepan and add the onions. Fry for 2 minutes, then cover, and turn the heat to low. Allow the onions to cook gently for 5 minutes, then remove the lid.

**2** Add the stock and herbs to the saucepan. Bring to a boil, then turn down the heat. Cover and simmer gently for 20 minutes.

**3** Remove the saucepan from the heat. Blend the soup with a hand blender or in a food processor or blender for about 15 seconds, until smooth. Alternatively, press it through a strainer with the back of a spoon. Return the soup to the saucepan.

**4** Reserve a little of the cheese for garnish. Spoon the remaining cheese into the soup and beat until the cheese is incorporated.

**5** Mix the cornstarch with the milk, then stir into the soup and heat, stirring constantly, until thickened and smooth.

**6** Pour the soup into 4 warmed bowls. Spoon some of the reserved cheese into each bowl and garnish with chives. Serve at once.

### SUMMER SOUP

In summer, this soup is wonderful when served chilled.

### HERBS

Choose at least two different types of herb for this soup, and make sure that one of them is quite mild, so that the flavor is not overpowering.

STEP 1

STEP 2

STEP 2

STEP 3

# LENTIL & PARSNIP POTAGE

*Smooth and delicious, this soup has the most glorious golden color and fabulous flavor.*

SERVES 4

*3 slices rindless bacon, chopped*
*1 onion, chopped*
*2 carrots, chopped*
*2 parsnips, chopped*
*1/3 cup red lentils*
*4 cups vegetable stock or*
  *water*
*salt and pepper*
*chopped fresh chives to garnish*

**1** Heat a large saucepan, add the bacon, and dry-fry for 5 minutes until crisp and golden.

**2** Add the onion, carrots, and parsnips and cook for about 5 minutes without browning.

**3** Add the lentils to the saucepan and stir to mix with the vegetables.

**4** Add the stock to the saucepan and bring to a boil. Cover and simmer for 30–40 minutes until tender.

**5** Transfer the soup to a blender or food processor and blend for about 15 seconds until smooth. Alternatively, press the soup through a strainer.

**6** Return to the saucepan and reheat gently until almost boiling. Season to taste. Garnish with chives and serve.

### VARIATIONS

Green or brown lentils can be used in place of the red ones. For more flavour, use 2 ham stock cubes instead of the vegetable stock or water.

### HAM

For a meatier soup which would make a good main course, use a leg of ham in place of the bacon. Cook it for 1 1/2–2 hours before adding the vegetables and lentils and use the ham's cooking liquid as the stock.

**STEP 1**

**STEP 2**

**STEP 3**

**STEP 4**

# LAMB & BARLEY BROTH

*Warming and nutritious, this broth is perfect for a cold winter's day.*
*The slow cooking allows you to use one of the cheaper cuts of meat.*

SERVES 4

1 tbsp vegetable oil
1 lb lamb neck slices
1 large onion, sliced
2 carrots, sliced
2 leeks, sliced
4 cups vegetable stock
1 bay leaf
few sprigs of fresh parsley
$^1/_3$ cup pearl barley

**1** Heat the oil in a large, heavy-based saucepan and add the pieces of lamb, turning them to seal and brown on both sides. Lift the lamb out of the pan and set aside.

**2** Add the onion, carrots, and leeks to the saucepan and cook gently for about 3 minutes.

**3** Return the lamb to the saucepan and add the stock, bay leaf, parsley, and pearl barley to the saucepan. Bring to a boil, then reduce the heat. Cover and simmer for 1½–2 hours until the lamb is tender.

**4** Discard the parsley sprigs. Lift the pieces of lamb from the broth and allow them to cool slightly. Remove the bones and any fat, and chop the meat. Return the lamb to the broth and reheat gently. Serve the broth in warmed bowls.

### TIPS

This broth will taste even better if made the day before, as this allows the flavors to fully develop. It also means that any fat will solidify on the surface so you can then lift it off. Keep the broth in the refrigerator until required.

### ONE-POT MEAL

If you like, make small dumplings and add them to the soup 20 minutes before serving for a more substantial meal.

# ITALIAN FISH STEW

*This wonderfully robust stew is full of fine Mediterranean flavors, such as basil, lemon, and tomato. As you can use any firm white fish, it's ideal for using whatever is the most economical.*

STEP 1

SERVES 4

2 tbsp olive oil
2 red onions, finely chopped
1 garlic clove, crushed
2 zucchini, sliced
14 oz can chopped tomatoes
3¹/₂ cups fish or vegetable
 stock
3 oz dried pasta shapes
12 oz firm white fish, such as cod, haddock,
 or hake
1 tbsp chopped fresh basil or oregano or
 1 tsp dried oregano
1 tsp grated lemon rind
1 tbsp cornstarch
1 tbsp water
salt and pepper
sprigs of fresh basil or oregano to garnish

STEP 2

**1** Heat the oil in a large saucepan and fry the onions and garlic for 5 minutes. Add the zucchini and cook for 2–3 minutes, stirring often.

**2** Add the tomatoes and stock to the saucepan and bring to the boil. Add the pasta, cover, and reduce the heat. Simmer for 5 minutes.

**3** Skin and bone the fish, then cut it into chunks. Add to the saucepan

STEP 3

with the basil or oregano, and lemon rind and cook gently for 5 minutes until the fish is opaque and flakes easily. Take care not to overcook it.

**4** Blend the cornstarch with the water and stir into the stew. Cook gently for 2 minutes, stirring, until thickened. Season to taste and ladle into 4 warmed soup bowls. Garnish with basil or oregano sprigs and serve at once.

### VARIATIONS

This recipe is a good way to use up a little leftover wine. Add one or two tablespoons of dry white wine just before serving.

Canned chopped tomatoes can be bought with a variety of flavorings; those with herbs are perfect for this stew.

STEP 4

**STEP 1**

**STEP 2**

**STEP 3**

**STEP 4**

# CHICKEN & CHILI BEAN POT

*This aromatic chicken dish has a spicy Mexican kick. Chicken thighs are not only more economical than breasts, they have much more flavor when cooked in this way.*

SERVES 4

*2 tbsp all-purpose flour*
*1 tsp chili powder*
*8 chicken thighs or 4 chicken legs*
*3 tbsp olive or vegetable oil*
*2 garlic cloves, crushed*
*1 large onion, chopped*
*1 green or red bell pepper, deseeded and*
*    chopped*
*1¼ cups chicken stock*
*12 oz tomatoes, chopped*
*14 oz can red kidney beans, rinsed and*
*    drained*
*2 tbsp tomato paste*
*salt and pepper*

**1** Mix together the flour, chili powder, and seasoning in a shallow dish. Rinse the chicken, but do not dry. Dip it into the seasoned flour, turning to coat it on all sides.

**2** Heat the oil in a large, deep skillet or saucepan and add the chicken. Cook over a high heat for 3–4 minutes, turning the pieces to brown them all over. Lift the chicken out of the skillet with a perforated spoon and drain on paper towels.

**3** Add the garlic, onion, and bell pepper to the skillet and cook for 2–3 minutes until softened.

**4** Add the stock, tomatoes, kidney beans, and tomato paste, stirring well. Bring to a boil, then return the chicken to the skillet. Reduce the heat and simmer, covered, for about 30 minutes, until the chicken is tender. Season to taste and serve at once.

### VARIATIONS

When fresh tomatoes are expensive, use a 14 oz can of chopped tomatoes instead.

Choose a mild, medium, or hot variety of chili powder, depending on your preference.

For extra intensity of flavor, use sun-dried tomato paste instead of ordinary tomato paste.

**STEP 1**

**STEP 2**

**STEP 3**

**STEP 4**

# BEEF GOULASH

*Slow, gentle cooking is the secret to this superb goulash – it really brings out the flavor of the ingredients.*

Serves 4

2 tbsp vegetable oil
1 large onion, chopped
1 garlic clove, crushed
1½ lb stewing beef, cut into chunks
2 tbsp paprika
14 oz can chopped tomatoes
2 tbsp tomato paste
1 large red bell pepper, deseeded and
  chopped
6 oz mushrooms, sliced
2½ cups beef stock
1 tbsp cornstarch
1 tbsp water
4 tbsp crème fraîche or natural yogurt
salt and pepper
paprika for sprinkling
chopped fresh parsley to garnish
long grain rice and wild rice to serve

**1** Heat the oil in a large skillet and cook the onion and garlic for 3–4 minutes, until softened. Add the meat and cook over a high heat for 3 minutes until browned all over.

**2** Add the paprika and stir well, then add the tomatoes, tomato paste, bell pepper, and mushrooms. Cook for 2 minutes, stirring frequently.

**3** Pour in the stock. Bring to a boil, then reduce the heat. Cover and simmer for 1½–2 hours until the meat is very tender.

**4** Blend the cornstarch with the water, then add to the skillet, stirring constantly until thickened and smooth. Cook for 1 minute, then season to taste.

**5** Put the crème fraîche or natural yogurt in a bowl and sprinkle with a little paprika. Garnish the goulash with chopped parsley and serve with rice and the crème fraîche or yogurt.

## PAPRIKA

Paprika is quite a mild, sweet spice, so you can add plenty without its being overpowering.

# CHAPTER TWO

# *Pies & Bakes*

The beauty of cooking on a budget is that you can benefit from the wonderful flavors of slow-cooked food. Tastes and textures mellow, often improving on recipes where food is more quickly cooked. In particular, it is a way of tenderizing cheaper cuts of meat which need gentle, moist cooking to make the most of them.

In this chapter, you'll find some cheap and cheerful ways to eat a hearty meal. Choose from Mariner's Pie (see page 26) – a tasty bake where the fish is 'stretched' by combining it with other basic ingredients. Or try Bacon, Onion, & Potato Hotpot (see page 32) – a surprisingly simple, delicious layered bake topped with crispy cooked bacon.

It's always a good idea to use all the available oven space when you are baking by cooking something else at the same time. It's one way of being energy-efficient and saving on fuel costs. You could even make double quantities of the chosen recipe, freezing some for future use. It hardly takes any longer to make two meals at once – and you'll have another at the ready when you next need it.

Opposite: *The extensive wheat fields of the United States.*

**STEP 1**

**STEP 2**

**STEP 3**

**STEP 4**

# BAKED STUFFED ONIONS

*Spanish onions are ideal for this recipe, as they have a milder, sweeter flavor that is not too overpowering.*

SERVES 4

4 large Spanish onions
2 slices rindless bacon, diced
½ red bell pepper, deseeded and diced
4 oz lean ground beef
1 tbsp chopped mixed fresh herbs such as
    parsley, thyme, and rosemary or
    1 tsp dried mixed herbs
½ cup fresh white breadcrumbs
1¼ cups beef stock
salt and pepper
chopped fresh parsley to garnish
long grain rice to serve

GRAVY:
2 tbsp butter
4 oz mushrooms, chopped finely
1¼ cups beef stock
2 tbsp cornstarch
2 tbsp water

**1** Put the onions in a saucepan of lightly salted water. Bring to a boil then simmer for 15 minutes until tender. Drain and cool slightly, then hollow out the centers and finely chop.

**2** Heat a skillet and cook the bacon until the fat runs. Add the chopped onion and bell pepper and cook for 5–7 minutes, stirring frequently. Add the beef and cook, stirring, for 3 minutes, until browned. Remove from the heat and stir in the herbs, breadcrumbs, and seasoning.

**3** Grease an ovenproof dish and stand the whole onions in it. Pack the beef mixture into the centers and pour the stock around them. Bake in a preheated oven at 350°F for 1–1½ hours until tender.

**4** To make the gravy, heat the butter in a small saucepan and fry the mushrooms for 3–4 minutes. Strain the liquid from the onions and add to the pan with the stock. Cook for 2–3 minutes. Mix the cornstarch with the water then stir into the gravy and heat, stirring, until thickened and smooth. Season. Serve the onions with the gravy and rice, garnished with parsley.

## VARIATION

Red, green, or yellow bell peppers are delicious used instead of onions, but don't pre-cook them, simply discard the cores and seeds. You will still need to used chopped onion in the filling, however.

STEP 1

STEP 2

STEP 3

STEP 4

# WINTER VEGETABLE COBBLER

*Seasonal fresh vegetables are casseroled with lentils then topped with a ring of fresh cheese biscuits to make this tasty cobbler.*

SERVES 4

1 tbsp olive oil
1 garlic clove, crushed
8 small onions, halved
2 celery stalks, sliced
8 oz rutabaga, chopped
2 carrots, sliced
$1/2$ small cauliflower, broken into
 flowerets
8 oz mushrooms, sliced
14 oz can chopped tomatoes
$1/4$ cup red lentils
2 tbsp cornstarch
3–4 tbsp water
$1 1/4$ cups vegetable stock
2 tsp Tabasco sauce
2 tsp chopped fresh oregano or parsley
oregano sprigs to garnish

COBBLER TOPPING:
2 cups self-rising flour
$1/4$ cup butter
1 cup grated sharp cheese
2 tsp chopped fresh oregano or parsley
1 egg, beaten
$2/3$ cup skim milk
salt

**1** Heat the oil in a large saucepan and fry the garlic and onions for 5 minutes. Add the celery, rutabaga, carrots, and cauliflower and fry for 2–3 minutes.

**2** Remove from the heat and add the mushrooms, tomatoes, and lentils. Mix the cornstarch with the water and add to the pan with the vegetable stock, Tabasco sauce, and oregano or parsley. Bring to a boil, stirring, until thickened. Transfer to an ovenproof dish, cover, and bake in a preheated oven at 350°F for 20 minutes.

**3** To make the topping, sift the flour and salt into a bowl. Rub in the butter, then stir in most of the cheese and the chopped herbs. Beat together the egg and milk and add enough to the dry ingredients to make a soft dough. Knead lightly, roll out to $1/2$ inch thick and cut into 2 inch rounds.

**4** Remove the casserole from the oven and increase the temperature to 400°F. Arrange the rounds around the edge of the dish, brush with the remaining egg and milk, and sprinkle with the reserved cheese. Cook for a further 10–12 minutes until the topping is risen and golden. Garnish and serve at once.

STEP 2

STEP 3

STEP 4

STEP 5

# MARINER'S PIE

*Make this cheap and nourishing fish pie with cod or any other inexpensive white fish.*

SERVES 4

*1½ lb potatoes*
*2 large leeks, sliced*
*1¼ cups + 2 tbsp milk*
*1 tbsp chopped fresh parsley*
*¼ cup butter*
*½ cup all-purpose flour*
*1½ lb skinned and boned cod or other white fish, cut into chunks*
*1 egg*
*salt and pepper*
*chopped fresh parsley to garnish*
*green beans and tomatoes to serve*

**1** Boil the potatoes in lightly salted water for about 15 minutes until tender. Meanwhile, cook the leeks in lightly salted boiling water for about 8 minutes.

**2** Drain the potatoes and leeks, reserving the cooking liquid. Mash the potatoes with 2 tbsp of the milk and half the butter until smooth. Make the remaining milk up to 2½ cups with the cooking liquid from the potatoes and leeks. Add the chopped parsley to the milk mixture.

**3** Melt the remaining butter in a saucepan. Add the flour and cook gently, stirring, for 1 minute. Gradually stir in the milk and parsley mixture. Heat, stirring constantly, until thickened and smooth. Season to taste.

**4** Grease a large, shallow ovenproof dish. Put the fish in the dish and arrange the cooked leeks on top. Pour over the parsley sauce.

**5** Pipe or spoon the potatoes on top. Bake in a preheated oven at 375°F for 25–30 minutes until golden. Garnish with parsley and serve with beans and tomatoes.

## VARIATIONS

For a treat, add a few cooked, peeled shrimp to the fish pie.

Top the pie with sliced potato if you prefer – cook the potatoes until just tender, then arrange on top of the pie, brushing with a little beaten egg and milk.

# GROUND LAMB & POTATO MOUSSAKA

*Ground lamb makes a very tasty and authentic moussaka. For a change, you could use ground beef.*

**SERVES 4**

1 large eggplant, sliced
1 tbsp olive or vegetable oil
1 onion, chopped finely
1 garlic clove, crushed
12 oz ground lamb
8 oz mushrooms, sliced
14 oz can chopped tomatoes with
  herbs
²/₃ cup lamb or vegetable stock
2 tbsp cornstarch
2 tbsp water
1 lb potatoes, parboiled for 10 minutes and
  sliced
2 eggs
¹/₂ cup low-fat soft cheese
²/₃ cup natural yogurt
¹/₂ cup grated sharp cheese
salt and pepper
flat-leaf parsley to garnish
green salad to serve

**1** Lay the eggplant slices on a clean surface and sprinkle liberally with salt, to extract the bitter juices. Leave for 10 minutes, then turn the slices over and repeat. Put in a colander, rinse, and drain well.

**2** Meanwhile, heat the oil in a saucepan and fry the onion and garlic for 3–4 minutes. Add the lamb and mushrooms and cook for 5 minutes, until browned. Stir in the tomatoes and stock, bring to a boil, and simmer for 10 minutes. Mix the cornstarch with the water and stir into the pan. Cook, stirring, until thickened.

**3** Spoon half the mixture into an ovenproof dish. Cover with the eggplant slices, then the remaining lamb mixture. Arrange the sliced potatoes on top.

**4** Beat together the eggs, soft cheese, yogurt, and seasoning. Pour over the potatoes to cover them completely. Sprinkle with the grated cheese.

**5** Bake in a preheated oven at 375°F for 45 minutes until the topping is set and golden brown. Garnish with flat-leaf parsley and serve with a green salad.

STEP 1

STEP 2

STEP 3

STEP 4

STEP 2

STEP 3

STEP 4

STEP 5

# SAVORY BATTER POPOVERS WITH THYME & ONION SAUCE

*A variation on pigs in blankets, these little popovers are filled with ground pork meatballs and served with a tasty thyme and onion sauce.*

SERVES 4

2 tbsp vegetable oil
1¹/₂ cups all-purpose flour
2 small eggs
scant 2 cups milk
salt and pepper
fresh thyme sprigs to garnish
leeks and carrots to serve

FILLING:
6 oz lean ground pork
1 very small onion, chopped finely
1 small carrot, grated finely
1 tbsp chopped fresh thyme or parsley
¹/₂ cup fresh whole wheat breadcrumbs

SAUCE:
1 tbsp vegetable oil
1 small onion, chopped finely
4 oz button mushrooms, sliced
1¹/₄ cups chicken or vegetable stock
1 tbsp chopped fresh thyme or parsley
2 tbsp cornstarch
2 tbsp water

**1** Spoon 2 teaspoons of the oil into each of 4 individual shallow ovenproof dishes.

**2** Whip together the flour, salt, eggs, and milk to make a smooth batter. Allow to stand while making the pork filling.

**3** To make the filling, mix together the pork, onion, carrot, thyme or parsley, breadcrumbs, and seasoning until thoroughly combined. Form the mixture into 12 small balls and place 3 in each dish. Bake in a preheated oven at 400°F for 10 minutes.

**4** Remove the dishes from the oven and quickly pour an equal amount of batter into each one. Bake for a further 20–25 minutes, until risen and golden brown.

**5** To make the sauce, heat the oil in a saucepan and fry the onion and mushrooms until browned. Add the stock and thyme or parsley. Bring to a boil, then reduce the heat, and simmer for 5 minutes. Mix the cornstarch with the water, stir into the pan, and heat, stirring, until the sauce boils and thickens. Garnish the popovers with thyme sprigs and serve with the sauce and vegetables.

STEP 1

STEP 2

STEP 3

STEP 5

# BACON, ONION, & POTATO HOTPOT

*Simple, straightforward, and satisfying, this old-fashioned casserole is perfect for chilly winter days.*

SERVES 4

*¹/₄ cup butter or margarine
2 lb large potatoes, sliced
1 lb onions, sliced
3¹/₂ cups chicken stock
1 lb rindless bacon slices
salt and pepper
broccoli to serve*

**1** Grease a 2 quart casserole with some of the butter or margarine. Layer the potatoes and onions alternately in the casserole dish, seasoning each layer with salt and pepper to taste. Finish with a layer of potato slices.

**2** Pour the stock over the potatoes and dot the surface with the remaining butter or margarine. Cover and bake in a preheated oven at 375°F for 45 minutes.

**3** Remove the lid from the casserole and return to the oven for a further 30 minutes until the potatoes are golden brown.

**4** Meanwhile, cook the bacon under a preheated moderate broiler until cooked, but not too crisp.

**5** Put the bacon on top of the potatoes and cook in the oven for a further 10 minutes. Serve at once on warmed plates, with broccoli.

## ACCOMPANIMENTS

As an alternative to broccoli, hot, buttered cabbage seasoned with a pinch of nutmeg tastes just right with this tasty, economical hotpot.

Homemade chutney or relish can also be served with this dish.

# *Pasta, Rice, & Grains*

Pasta, grains, rice, and noodles are the carbohydrate foods that fill us up and provide the slow release of energy that gets us through the day. Gone are the days when people thought these starchy foods were fattening. Now people realize that carbohydrates – the fuel store in plants – can be our own fuel supply too, so foods such as pasta, potatoes, grains, and rice form an important basic item for each and every one of our meals.

In themselves, these foods are quite bland, which means that they can so easily take on the flavors and characteristics of many different meals. Think of the innumerable ways in which the Italians serve pasta, for example. This chapter will show you a little of the versatility of these foods, so you can continue to experiment in your own kitchen and develop some ideas of your own.

Opposite: *A view over Florence, Italy, dominated by the magnificent dome of the cathedral.*

**STEP 1**

**STEP 2**

**STEP 3**

**STEP 4**

# THAI-STYLE CHICKEN FRIED RICE

*A few authentic ingredients give this spicy rice dish a typically Thai flavor.*

SERVES 4

*generous 1 cup long-grain rice*
*4 tbsp vegetable oil*
*2 garlic cloves, chopped finely*
*6 shallots, sliced finely*
*1 red bell pepper, deseeded and diced*
*4 oz green beans, cut into 1 inch*
  *lengths*
*1 tbsp Thai red curry paste*
*12 oz cooked chicken, chopped*
*1/2 tsp ground coriander*
*1 tsp finely grated ginger root*
*2 tbsp Thai fish sauce*
*finely grated rind of 1 lime*
*3 tbsp lime juice*
*1 tbsp chopped fresh cilantro*
*salt and pepper*

*TO GARNISH:*
*lime wedges*
*fresh cilantro sprigs*

**1** Cook the rice in plenty of boiling, lightly salted water for 12–15 minutes until tender. Drain, rinse in cold water, and drain thoroughly.

**2** Heat the oil in a large skillet or wok and add the garlic and shallots. Fry gently for 2–3 minutes until golden.

**3** Add the red bell pepper and green beans and stir-fry for 2 minutes. Add the Thai curry paste and stir-fry for 1 minute.

**4** Add the cooked rice to the skillet or wok, then add the chicken, ground coriander, ginger, fish sauce, lime rind and juice, and fresh cilantro. Stir-fry over a medium-high heat for about 4–5 minutes, until the rice and chicken are thoroughly reheated. Season to taste.

**5** Garnish with lime wedges and cilantro and serve.

### THAI RED CURRY PASTE

Thai red curry paste can be bought in small jars in supermarkets and delicatessens. Look for it in the Oriental foods section.

### THAI FISH SAUCE

Thai fish sauce is used to season many Thai dishes. It adds a salty flavor, rather than a seafood one, so take care when adding extra salt to the dish. Use light soy sauce as an alternative.

STEP 1

STEP 2

STEP 3

STEP 4

# MUSHROOM & PARMESAN RISOTTO

*Make this creamy risotto with Italian risotto rice and freshly grated Parmesan cheese for the best results.*

SERVES 4

*2 tbsp olive or vegetable oil*
*generous 1 cup risotto rice*
*2 garlic cloves, crushed*
*1 onion, chopped*
*2 celery stalks, chopped*
*1 red or green bell pepper, deseeded and*
*    chopped*
*8 oz mushrooms, sliced*
*1 tbsp chopped fresh oregano or 1 tsp dried*
*    oregano*
*4 cups vegetable stock*
*2 oz sun-dried tomatoes in olive oil, drained*
*    and chopped (optional)*
*1/2 cup finely grated Parmesan cheese*
*salt and pepper*

*TO GARNISH:*
*fresh flat-leaf parsley sprigs*
*fresh bay leaves*

**1** Heat the oil in a wok or large skillet. Add the rice and cook, stirring, for 5 minutes.

**2** Add the garlic, onion, celery, and bell pepper and cook, stirring, for 5 minutes. Add the mushrooms and cook for a further 3–4 minutes.

**3** Stir in the oregano and stock. Heat until just boiling, then reduce the heat, cover, and simmer gently for about 20 minutes until the rice is tender and creamy.

**4** Add the sun-dried tomatoes, if using, and season to taste. Stir in half the Parmesan cheese. Top with the remaining cheese, garnish with flat-leaf parsley and bay leaves, and serve.

### RISOTTO RICE

This is an Italian short-grain rice used specially for risottos – the starch it contains is essential for the creamy texture, so don't rinse it before cooking.
   Check the rice as it cooks from time to time. If it has absorbed all the liquid before it is tender, add a little extra stock or water.

### OIL

Use the oil from the sun-dried tomatoes to fry the rice to give it extra flavor.

# PASTA WITH PINE KERNELS & BLUE CHEESE

*Simple, quick, and inexpensive, this tasty pasta dish can be prepared in minutes.*

STEP 1

**SERVES 4**

*1 cup pine kernels*
*12 oz dried pasta shapes*
*2 zucchini, sliced*
*4 oz broccoli, broken into flowerets*
*1 cup full-fat soft cheese*
*²/₃ cup milk*
*1 tbsp chopped fresh basil*
*4 oz button mushrooms, sliced*
*3 oz blue cheese, crumbled*
*salt and pepper*
*sprigs of fresh basil to garnish*
*green salad to serve*

**1** Scatter the pine kernels onto a cookie sheet and broil, turning occasionally, until lightly browned all over. Set aside.

**2** Cook the pasta in plenty of boiling, lightly salted water for 8–10 minutes until it is just tender. Meanwhile, cook the zucchini and broccoli in a small amount of boiling, lightly salted water for about 5 minutes until just tender.

**3** Put the soft cheese into a saucepan and heat gently, stirring constantly. Add the milk and stir to mix.

**4** Add the basil and mushrooms and cook gently for 2–3 minutes. Stir in the blue cheese and season to taste.

**5** Drain the pasta and the vegetables and mix together. Pour over the cheese and mushroom sauce and add the pine kernels. Toss gently to mix. Garnish with basil sprigs and serve on warmed plates with a green salad.

STEP 2

STEP 3

### PASTA

Avoid overcooking pasta; it should retain a little 'bite' (known as 'al dente' in Italian).

### LOW-FAT VERSION

Use low-fat soft cheese instead of full-fat soft cheese if you want to reduce the calories and fat of this recipe.

STEP 4

**STEP 1**

**STEP 2**

**STEP 3**

**STEP 4**

# SMOKED FISH LASAGNE

*Use smoked cod or haddock in this delicious lasagne. It's a great way to make a little go a long way.*

SERVES 4

2 tsp olive or vegetable oil
1 garlic clove, crushed
1 small onion, chopped finely
4 oz mushrooms, sliced
14 oz can chopped tomatoes
1 small zucchini, sliced
²/₃ cup vegetable stock or water
2 tbsp butter or margarine
1¼ cups skim milk
¼ cup all-purpose flour
1 cup grated sharp cheese
1 tbsp chopped fresh parsley
6 sheets pre-cooked lasagne
12 oz skinned and boned smoked cod or
    haddock, cut into chunks
salt and pepper
fresh parsley sprigs to garnish

**1** Heat the oil in a saucepan and fry the garlic and onion for about 5 minutes. Add the mushrooms and cook for 3 minutes.

**2** Add the tomatoes, zucchini, and stock or water and simmer, uncovered, for 15–20 minutes until the vegetables are soft. Season.

**3** Put the butter or margarine, milk, and flour into a small saucepan and heat, beating constantly, until the sauce boils and thickens. Remove from the heat and add half the cheese and all the parsley. Stir gently to melt the cheese and season to taste.

**4** Spoon the tomato sauce mixture into a large, shallow ovenproof dish and top with half the lasagne sheets. Scatter the chunks of fish evenly over the top, then pour over half the cheese sauce. Top with the remaining lasagne sheets and spread the rest of the cheese sauce on top. Sprinkle with the remaining cheese.

**5** Bake in a preheated oven at 375°F for 40 minutes, until the top is golden brown and bubbling. Garnish with parsley sprigs and serve.

### BUYING FISH

Look out for bargains at your fish store, and substitute whatever fish is cheapest. Firm white fish is particularly suitable for this recipe.

STEP 1

STEP 2

STEP 3

STEP 4

# QUICK CHINESE CHICKEN WITH NOODLES

*Chicken and fresh vegetables are flavored with ginger and Chinese five-spice powder in this speedy stir-fry.*

**SERVES 4**

6 oz Chinese thread egg noodles
2 tbsp sesame or vegetable oil
¼ cup peanuts
1 bunch of scallions, sliced
1 green bell pepper, deseeded and cut into
    thin strips
1 large carrot, cut into strips
4 oz cauliflower, broken into small
    flowerets
12 oz skinless, boneless chicken, cut into
    strips
8 oz mushrooms, sliced
1 tsp finely grated ginger root
1 tsp Chinese five-spice powder
1 tbsp chopped fresh cilantro
1 tbsp light soy sauce
salt and pepper
fresh chives to garnish

**1** Put the noodles into a large bowl and cover with boiling water. Leave to soak for 6 minutes, or according to packet instructions.

**2** Meanwhile, heat the oil in a wok or large skillet. Add the peanuts and stir-fry for about 1 minute until browned. Lift them out with a perforated spoon and drain on paper towels.

**3** Add the scallions, bell pepper, carrot, cauliflower, and chicken to the wok or skillet. Stir-fry over a high heat for 4–5 minutes, until the chicken is cooked. The vegetables should remain crisp and colorful.

**4** Drain the noodles thoroughly and add them to the wok or skillet. Add the mushrooms and stir-fry for 2 minutes. Add the ginger, five-spice powder, and cilantro and stir-fry for 1 further minute.

**5** Season with soy sauce and salt and pepper. Sprinkle with the peanuts, garnish with chives, and serve on warmed plates.

## VARIATIONS

Instead of ginger root, 1/2 teaspoon ground ginger can be used.
    Vary the vegetables according to what is in season. Make the most of bargains bought from your local store or market.

**STEP 1**

**STEP 2**

**STEP 3**

**STEP 4**

# MOROCCAN VEGETABLE COUSCOUS

*Couscous is a semolina grain which is very quick to cook, and it makes a pleasant change from rice or pasta.*

SERVES 4

2 tbsp vegetable oil
1 large onion, chopped coarsely
1 carrot, chopped
1 turnip, chopped
2¹/₂ cups vegetable stock
1 cup couscous
2 tomatoes, skinned and quartered
2 zucchini, chopped
1 red bell pepper, deseeded and chopped
4 oz green beans, chopped
grated rind of 1 lemon
pinch of ground turmeric (optional)
1 tbsp finely chopped fresh cilantro or
    parsley
salt and pepper
fresh flat-leaf parsley sprigs to garnish

**1** Heat the oil in a large saucepan and fry the onion, carrot, and turnip for 3–4 minutes. Add the vegetable stock and bring to the boil. Cover and simmer gently for about 20 minutes.

**2** Meanwhile, put the couscous in a bowl and moisten with a little boiling water, stirring, until the grains have swollen and separated.

**3** Add the tomatoes, zucchini, bell pepper, and green beans to the saucepan.

**4** Stir the lemon rind and turmeric, if using, into the couscous and mix well. Put the couscous in a steamer and position over the vegetables. Simmer the vegetables so that the couscous steams for 8–10 minutes.

**5** Pile the couscous onto warmed serving plates. Ladle the vegetables and some of the liquid on top. Scatter with the cilantro or parsley and serve at once, garnished with parsley sprigs.

### VARIATION

For a tasty chicken couscous, cook 4 chicken portions with the vegetables in step 1, adding extra stock to cover.

### TIP

Add extra stock to the vegetables if the saucepan begins to boil dry.

# CHAPTER FOUR

# *Eggs & Cheese*

Eggs and cheese are the two great staple foods of low-cost cookery. High in protein yet relatively inexpensive, they can form the foundation of many tasty budget meals.

Eggs are so versatile. From simple boiled, poached, scrambled, and fried eggs you can progress to quick and tasty omelets through to light and impressive soufflés. Eggs form one of the vital ingredients in many basic recipes – batter, choux pastry, and custards to name but a few.

With the recipes in this chapter, for example, you can rustle up Savory Bread & Butter Bake (see page 52) in a matter of moments for a speedy mid-week meal – the hot melting cheese makes your mouth water as the dish emerges from the oven, all puffed-up and golden brown. Or try Egg & Garbanzo Bean Curry (see page 50) – the subtle spices will soon perk up your appetite!

Opposite: *A cheese market in Holland. The whole cheeses are still transported in the traditional way.*

STEP 1

STEP 2

STEP 3

STEP 4

# EGG & GARBANZO BEAN CURRY

*This easy vegetarian curry is always enjoyed. Double the quantities and it's a great dish if you're cooking for a crowd.*

SERVES 4

2 tbsp vegetable oil
2 garlic cloves, crushed
1 large onion, chopped
1 large carrot, sliced
1 apple, cored and chopped
2 tbsp medium-hot curry powder
1 tsp finely grated fresh ginger root
2 tsp paprika
3½ cups vegetable stock
2 tbsp tomato paste
½ small cauliflower, broken into flowerets
15 oz can garbanzo beans, rinsed and
    drained
2 tbsp golden raisins
2 tbsp cornstarch
2 tbsp water
4 hard-cooked eggs, quartered
salt and pepper
paprika to garnish

CUCUMBER DIP:
3 inch piece of cucumber, chopped finely
1 tbsp chopped fresh mint
⅔ cup natural yogurt
sprigs of fresh mint to garnish

**1** Heat the oil in a large saucepan and fry the garlic, onion, carrot, and apple for 4–5 minutes, until softened.

**2** Add the curry powder, ginger, and paprika and fry for 1 further minute.

**3** Stir in the vegetable stock and tomato paste.

**4** Add the cauliflower, garbanzo beans, and raisins. Bring to a boil, then reduce the heat, and simmer, covered, for 25–30 minutes until the vegetables are tender.

**5** Blend the cornstarch with the water and add to the curry, stirring until thickened. Cook gently for 2 minutes. Season to taste.

**6** To make the dip, in a small serving bowl, mix together the cucumber, mint, and yogurt.

**7** Ladle the curry onto 4 warmed serving plates and arrange the eggs on top. Sprinkle with a little paprika. Garnish the cucumber and mint dip with mint and serve with the curry.

**STEP 1**

**STEP 2**

**STEP 3**

**STEP 4**

# SAVORY BREAD &
# BUTTER BAKE

*Quick, simple, and nutritious – what more could you ask for an
inexpensive mid-week meal?*

SERVES **4**

*¼ cup butter or margarine*
*1 bunch scallions, sliced*
*6 slices of white or brown bread, crusts
    removed*
*1½ cups grated sharp cheese*
*2 eggs*
*scant 2 cups milk*
*salt and pepper*
*fresh flat-leaf parsley sprigs to garnish*

**1** Grease a 1½ quart baking dish with
a little of the butter or margarine.
Melt the remaining butter or margarine
in a small saucepan and gently fry the
scallions until softened and golden.

**2** Meanwhile, cut the bread into
triangles and layer half of them in
the baking dish. Top with the scallions
and half the cheese.

**3** Beat together the eggs and milk
and season with salt and pepper.
Layer the remaining triangles of bread in
the dish and carefully pour over the milk
mixture. Leave to soak for 15–20
minutes.

**4** Sprinkle the remaining cheese over
the soaked bread. Bake in a
preheated oven at 375°F for 35–40
minutes until puffed up and golden
brown. Garnish with flat-leaf parsley and
serve at once.

### BREAD

This is an excellent recipe for using up
bread that is slightly stale.

### VARIATIONS

For a change, add ⅓ cup chopped cooked
ham to the scallions, when layering them
in the baking dish.
    Use 1 large onion instead of the
scallions, if preferred.

# SPINACH & CHEESE PANCAKE STACK

*Make a pile of pancakes, then bake them with a wonderful filling for a satisfying and nutritious meal.*

STEP 1

**SERVES 4**

1 cup all-purpose flour
1 egg
1¼ cups milk
2 tbsp vegetable oil
salt and pepper
fresh flat-leaf parsley sprigs to garnish
mixed salad to serve

*FILLING:*
1 lb fresh spinach, washed
   thoroughly
1 onion, chopped
2 garlic cloves, crushed
14 oz can chopped tomatoes
1 tsp mixed dried Italian herbs
1 cup grated sharp cheese

**1** Sift the flour and a pinch of salt into a large bowl. Add the egg and milk and beat together to make a smooth batter.

**2** Reserve 1 tablespoon of the oil. Heat a large heavy-based skillet and make 4 pancakes with the batter, using a few drops of oil to make each one. Stack the pancakes on a plate once they are cooked.

**3** To make the filling, pack the spinach into a large saucepan and add a little salted water. Cover and cook for 4–5 minutes, then drain well, and squeeze out the excess liquid.

**4** Heat the reserved oil in a skillet and fry the onion and garlic for 5 minutes. Add the tomatoes and cook for about 10 minutes until pulpy. Add the mixed herbs and season with salt and pepper to taste.

**5** Brush a 9 inch deep cake pan with the remaining oil.

**6** Layer the pancakes, spinach, and tomato mixture in the pan, finishing with a pancake. Scatter the cheese evenly over the surface and bake in a preheated oven at 375°F for 30 minutes until golden brown. Slice into wedges, garnish, and serve hot with a mixed salad.

## VARIATIONS

Use whole wheat flour instead of white flour for the pancakes.

Add some sliced mushrooms to the tomato mixture if you wish.

STEP 2

STEP 3

STEP 4

STEP 1

STEP 2

STEP 4

STEP 5

# CHICKEN & CORN PUFF

*This delicious choux puff is an impressive dish yet it's simple to make.*
*You can use the choux pastry as a topping for all kinds of filling.*

SERVES 4

CHOUX PASTRY:
generous ¹/₂ cup all-purpose flour
¹/₄ cup butter or margarine
²/₃ cup water
2 eggs, beaten
salt

FILLING:
2 tbsp butter or margarine
¹/₄ cup all-purpose flour
1¹/₄ cups skim milk
1 cup shredded cooked chicken
³/₄ cup canned corn, drained
1 tbsp chopped fresh parsley
salt and pepper

**1** To make the choux pastry, sift the flour and salt into a bowl. Put the butter or margarine and water into a saucepan, then heat gently to melt. Bring to a boil. Remove from the heat and quickly add the flour all at once. Beat with a wooden spoon until the mixture leaves the sides of the saucepan clean. Leave to cool slightly.

**2** Gradually beat in the eggs, using an electric mixer if wished, until the mixture is thick and very glossy. Chill while making the filling.

**3** To make the filling, put the butter or margarine, flour, and milk into a saucepan. Heat, beating constantly, until smooth and thickened.

**4** Add the chicken, corn, and parsley to the sauce. Season to taste. Pour into a 4 cup shallow baking dish.

**5** Spoon the choux pastry around the edge of the dish. Bake in a preheated oven at 425°F for 35–40 minutes until puffed up and golden brown. Serve at once.

## CHOUX PASTRY

For successful choux pastry, it is important to measure the ingredients accurately. Make sure the mixture has cooled before beating in the eggs, or they could curdle.

STEP 1

STEP 3

STEP 4

STEP 5

# GOLDEN CHEESE & LEEK
# POTATO PATTIES

*Make these tasty potato patties for a quick and simple supper dish.
Serve them with scrambled eggs if you're very hungry.*

SERVES 4

2 lb potatoes
4 tbsp milk
¼ cup butter or margarine
2 leeks, chopped finely
1 onion, chopped finely
1½ cups grated white, semi-hard
  cheese
1 tbsp chopped fresh parsley or chives
1 egg, beaten
2 tbsp water
1½ cups fresh white or brown
  breadcrumbs
vegetable oil for shallow frying
salt and pepper
fresh flat-leaf parsley sprigs to garnish
mixed salad to serve

**1** Cook the potatoes in lightly salted boiling water until tender. Drain and mash them with the milk and the butter or margarine.

**2** Cook the leeks and onion in a small amount of salted boiling water for about 10 minutes until tender. Drain.

**3** In a large mixing bowl, combine the leeks and onion with the mashed potato, cheese, and parsley or chives. Season to taste.

**4** Beat together the egg and water in a shallow bowl. Sprinkle the breadcrumbs into a separate shallow bowl. Shape the potato mixture into 12 even-sized patties brushing each with the egg mixture, then coating with the breadcrumbs.

**5** Heat the oil in a large skillet and fry the potato patties gently for about 2–3 minutes on each side until light golden brown. Garnish with flat-leaf parsley and serve with a mixed salad.

### FISH PATTIES

Transform these potato patties into tasty fish patties by mixing in a 7 oz can of tuna, drained and flaked.

### POTATOES

This is an excellent recipe for using up leftover mashed potatoes.

**STEP 1**

**STEP 2**

**STEP 3**

**STEP 4**

# FLAMENCO EGGS

*This Spanish-style egg recipe is full of lively colors and flavors. Eating on a budget need never be dull.*

SERVES 4

6 tbsp olive oil
2 thick slices white bread, cut into cubes
1 lb potatoes, cut into small cubes
1 onion, chopped
2 oz green beans, cut into 1 inch lengths
2 small zucchini, halved and sliced
1 red bell pepper, deseeded and chopped
4 tomatoes, deseeded and sliced
2 chorizo or garlic sausages, sliced
chili powder, to taste
4 eggs
salt
chopped fresh parsley to garnish

**1** Heat the oil in a large skillet and add the cubes of bread. Fry until golden brown, then remove with a perforated spoon and drain on paper towels. Set aside.

**2** Add the potatoes to the skillet and cook over a low heat, turning often, for about 15 minutes until just tender.

**3** Add the onion to the skillet and cook for 3 minutes, then add the green beans, zucchini, bell pepper, and tomatoes. Cook gently for 3–4 minutes, stirring often. Stir in the chorizo sausage or garlic sausage. Season with salt and a little chili powder.

**4** Grease 4 individual ovenproof dishes or 1 large ovenproof dish with olive oil. Transfer the vegetable mixture to the dishes and make a hollow in the mixture. Carefully crack 1 egg into each hollow. Bake in a preheated oven at 375°F for 10 minutes.

**5** Sprinkle the cubes of fried bread over the surface and bake for a further 2 minutes. Serve immediately, garnished with chopped fresh parsley.

### CHILI POWDER

If you don't like the heat of chili powder, use freshly ground black pepper instead.

### TIP

Slightly stale bread is best for making the fried bread cubes, as it absorbs less oil.

# CHAPTER FIVE

# *Desserts*

This chapter is for everyone who feels that they haven't finished a meal properly until they have eaten dessert. And why not? Puddings are such a delight and great for filling any gaps. Lots of people prefer not to eat puddings, believing them to be stodgy and unhealthy, but this need not be the case. The key to a healthy, balanced diet is moderation, which doesn't mean banning foods that you love to eat. Every now and again a delicious dessert can be just what you need to feel comforted and cozy.

As with all the ideas in this book, the recipes have been developed with cost-cutting in mind. The recipes use basic, store-cupboard foods or ingredients that can easily be bought locally – nothing exotic or expensive. And there is nothing complicated in the preparation either – the desserts are quick and simple to prepare, which means that they are just right for any occasion. So whether it's for a family lunch or a special party, you can be sure that these desserts will go down a treat.

Opposite: *Fresh fruits are so packed with flavor you don't need to add lots of other ingredients to make mouthwatering desserts.*

STEP 1

STEP 2

STEP 3

STEP 4

# CHOCOLATE BREAD PUDDING

*This chocolate pudding is served with hot fudge sauce, making it the
most delicious way to use up bread that is slightly stale.*

SERVES 4

6 thick slices white bread, crusts
  removed
2 cups milk
6 oz can evaporated milk
2 tbsp unsweetened cocoa powder
2 eggs
2 tbsp dark brown sugar
1 tsp vanilla extract
confectioners' sugar for dusting

HOT FUDGE SAUCE:
2 squares dark chocolate, broken into pieces
1 tbsp unsweetened cocoa powder
2 tbsp light corn syrup
$^{1}/_{4}$ cup butter or margarine
2 tbsp dark brown sugar
$^{2}/_{3}$ cup milk
1 tbsp cornstarch

**1** Grease a shallow ovenproof dish.
Cut the bread into squares and
layer them in the dish.

**2** Heat the milk, evaporated milk,
and cocoa powder until lukewarm,
stirring occasionally.

**3** Beat together the eggs, sugar, and
vanilla extract. Add the warm milk
mixture and beat well.

**4** Pour into the baking dish, making
sure that all the bread is covered.
Cover the dish with plastic wrap and chill
for 1–2 hours.

**5** Bake the pudding in a preheated
oven at 350°F for about 35–40
minutes until set. Allow to stand for 5
minutes.

**6** To make the sauce, put the
chocolate, cocoa powder, syrup,
butter or margarine, sugar, milk, and
cornstarch into a saucepan. Heat gently,
stirring until smooth.

**7** Dust the pudding with
confectioners' sugar and serve with
the hot fudge sauce.

TIPS

The bread can be left to soak in the
chocolate mixture for several hours, or
overnight, if preferred.

STEP 1

STEP 2

STEP 3

STEP 4

# QUICK SYRUP SPONGE

*You won't believe your eyes when you see how quickly this sponge pudding cooks!*

**SERVES 4**

*¹/₂ cup butter or margarine*
*4 tbsp light corn syrup*
*¹/₃ cup superfine sugar*
*2 eggs*
*1 cup self-rising flour*
*1 tsp baking powder*
*about 2 tbsp warm water*
*custard to serve*

**1** Grease a 1½ quart pudding mold with a small amount of the butter or margarine. Spoon the syrup into the mold.

**2** Cream the remaining butter or margarine with the sugar until light and fluffy. Gradually add the eggs, beating well between each addition.

**3** Sift the flour and baking powder together, then fold into the creamed mixture using a large metal spoon. Add enough water to give a soft, dropping consistency. Spoon into the pudding mold and level the surface.

**4** Cover with microwave-safe plastic wrap, leaving a small space to allow air to escape. Microwave on Full Power for 4 minutes, then remove from the microwave and allow the pudding to stand for 5 minutes, while it continues to cook.

**5** Turn the pudding out onto a serving plate. Serve with custard.

### STEAMING

If you don't have a microwave, this pudding can be steamed. Cover the pudding with a piece of pleated baking parchment, then a piece of pleated foil, secure with string and place in a large saucepan. Add enough boiling water to come halfway up the sides of the mold, cover and steam for 1½ hours, topping up with more boiling water as necessary.

### LIGHT CORN SYRUP

Warm the spoon that you use to measure out the syrup and the syrup will slip off the spoon quite easily.
Use your favorite jelly in place of light corn syrup for a change.

STEP 1

STEP 2

STEP 3

STEP 4

# PANCAKES WITH APPLES & BUTTERSCOTCH SAUCE

*The sharpness of the apples contrasts with the sweetness of the sauce in this mouthwatering pancake recipe.*

**SERVES 4**

1 cup all-purpose flour
1 tsp finely grated lemon rind
1 egg
1¼ cups milk
1–2 tbsp vegetable oil
salt
pared lemon rind to garnish

FILLING:
8 oz tart apples, peeled, cored and
    sliced
2 tbsp golden raisins

SAUCE:
⅓ cup butter
3 tbsp light corn syrup
½ cup light muscovado sugar
1 tbsp rum or brandy (optional)
1 tbsp lemon juice

**1** Sift the flour and salt into a large mixing bowl. Add the lemon rind, egg, and milk and beat together to make a smooth batter.

**2** Heat a few drops of oil in a heavy-based skillet. Make 8 thin pancakes, using a few drops of oil for each one. Stack the cooked pancakes, layering them with paper towels.

**3** To make the filling, cook the apples with the golden raisins in a little water until soft. Divide the mixture between the pancakes and roll up or fold into triangles. Place them in a buttered ovenproof dish and bake in a preheated oven at 325°F for 15 minutes to warm through.

**4** To make the sauce, melt the butter, syrup, and sugar together in a saucepan, stirring well. Add the rum or brandy, if using, and the lemon juice  Do not allow the mixture to boil.

**5** Serve the pancakes on warm plates, with a little sauce poured over and garnished with lemon rind.

### TIPS

If the apples are too tart, sweeten them with a little sugar.
    To make thin pancakes, tilt the skillet as the batter is added, so that it flows quickly over the base.

**STEP 1**

**STEP 4**

**STEP 5**

**STEP 6**

# APRICOT & BANANA QUEEN OF PUDDINGS

*A scrumptious version of a classic British pudding.*

Serves 4

2 cups fresh white breadcrumbs
2¹/₂ cups milk
3 eggs
¹/₂ tsp vanilla extract
¹/₄ cup superfine sugar
2 bananas
1 tbsp lemon juice
3 tbsp apricot jelly

**1** Sprinkle the breadcrumbs into a 4 cup ovenproof dish. Heat the milk until lukewarm, then pour it over the breadcrumbs.

**2** Separate 2 of the eggs and beat the yolks with the remaining whole egg. Add to the baking dish with the vanilla extract and half the sugar, stirring well to mix. Allow to stand for 10 minutes.

**3** Bake in a preheated oven at 350°F for 40 minutes until set. Remove from the oven.

**4** Slice the bananas and sprinkle with the lemon juice. Spoon the apricot jelly onto the pudding and spread out to cover the surface. Arrange the bananas on top of the apricot jelly.

**5** Beat the egg whites until stiff, then add the remaining sugar. Beat until very stiff and glossy.

**6** Pile on top of the pudding, return to the oven and cook for a further 10–15 minutes until set and golden brown. Serve immediately.

### MERINGUE

The meringue will have a soft, marshmallow-like texture, unlike a hard meringue which is cooked slowly for 2–3 hours until dry.

Always use a grease-free bowl and whisk for beating egg-whites, otherwise they will not whip properly.

# BAKED SEMOLINA PUDDING WITH SPICED PLUMS

*Plums simmered in orange juice and mixed spice complement this semolina pudding perfectly.*

STEP 1

SERVES 4

2 tbsp butter or margarine
2¹/₂ cups milk
finely pared rind and juice of 1 orange
¹/₃ cup semolina
pinch of grated nutmeg
2 tbsp superfine sugar
1 egg, beaten

TO SERVE:
1 tsp butter
grated nutmeg

SPICED PLUMS:
8 oz plums, halved and pitted
²/₃ cup orange juice
2 tbsp superfine sugar
¹/₂ tsp ground mixed spice

**1** Grease a 4 cup ovenproof dish with a little of the butter or margarine. Put the milk, the remaining butter or margarine, and the orange rind in a saucepan. Sprinkle in the semolina and heat until boiling, stirring constantly. Simmer gently for 2–3 minutes. Remove from the heat.

**2** Add the nutmeg, orange juice, and sugar to the semolina mixture, stirring well. Add the egg and stir to mix.

**3** Transfer the mixture to the prepared dish and bake in a preheated oven at 375°F for about 30 minutes until lightly browned.

**4** To make the spiced plums, put the plums, orange juice, sugar, and spice into a saucepan and simmer gently for about 10 minutes until just tender. Leave to cool slightly.

**5** Top the semolina pudding with the butter and grated nutmeg and serve with the spiced plums.

STEP 2

STEP 3

VARIATION

Stewed apples make a delicious alternative to plums.

TIP

If you are short of time, there is no need to bake the pudding. Just reheat it gently, stirring constantly, after adding the egg.

STEP 4

73

STEP 1

STEP 2

STEP 3

STEP 4

# COFFEE CREAM TRIFLE

*Make the most of leftover ginger cake with this wonderful English trifle that's perfect for a special occasion.*

SERVES 6

6 oz ginger cake, sliced
3 tbsp coffee essence
5 tbsp hot water
4 tbsp dark rum
1/3 cup cornstarch
3 tbsp light muscovado sugar
1 tbsp butter or margarine
2 1/2 cups milk
2/3 cup heavy cream

TO DECORATE:
1 tbsp brown crystal sugar
grated chocolate
flaked almonds

**1** Arrange the slices of ginger cake in the base of a glass serving dish. Mix together the coffee essence, water, and rum. Pour half the mixture over the ginger cake.

**2** Put the cornstarch, sugar, butter or margarine, and milk in a saucepan. Heat gently, beating constantly until thickened and smooth. Cook gently for 2 minutes. Remove from the heat.

**3** Add the remaining coffee mixture, stirring well to blend. Pour over the ginger cake. Allow to cool completely.

**4** In a large chilled bowl, whip the cream until it holds its shape. Spoon into a large piping bag fitted with a star tip.

**5** Pipe swirls of cream around the edge of the trifle. Sprinkle with brown crystal sugar and decorate with grated chocolate and flaked almonds.

### VARIATIONS

Use plain sponge cake instead of ginger cake, if preferred.

To make this trifle more economical, use 2 teaspoons rum flavoring in place of the rum.

# KEEPING TO A BUDGET

**BAKING CAKES**
Some of the costliest items to buy are the snacks, cookies, cakes, bakes, and puddings that are so tempting, and that make great fillers when you're feeling hungry. So if you enjoy eating them, you're sure to enjoy making them too. Set aside an afternoon when you can batch-bake some cakes to eat over a few weeks, and keep them well-wrapped in an airtight container or freeze them until you need them.

If you are batch-baking, it is best to choose cakes that need the same oven temperature, so that you are making the most economical use of both your time and the oven heat.

Make lots of snack foods for the children; perfect for picnics and lunches. They will love homemade flapjacks and cookies, and they will be far cheaper than bought varieties or snack bars and chocolate.

Homemade pie dough is much cheaper than the bought variety, but it can get tedious if you have to make it each time you want to use it. Why not do the rubbing in for several batches of basic pie dough at once, then bag them in portions. You can keep them in the refrigerator for 3–4 weeks, or freeze them for 3 months.

Cooking on a budget can be quite a challenge – it's not an easy task making the money stretch when everything is so expensive. Yet there are many ways to cut down on your expenditure, once you've got into the swing of watching the family budget!

The most important aspect of low-cost cookery is to make sure that you and your family eat well and wisely. There is no gain in saving money if it means that your health and wellbeing are going to suffer. So any attempts to cut the food budget must not jeopardize the main reason for eating food. We must always provide our bodies with everything that they require to function as efficiently as possible and give us the energy we need.

Good nutrition is at the core of cooking on a budget. All the recipes have been devised with healthy eating in mind, so that they help to provide the body with the nutrients that are needed.

Luckily, economical meals don't have to be boring. Tasty, imaginative food can be very inexpensive. You can make the most marvelous meals with fresh, seasonal vegetables and fruit, cheaper cuts of meat and poultry, and less expensive types of fish. If you buy wisely you can save lots of money, but first it's a good idea to assess your shopping habits.

**Buying wisely**
Think about the way you buy food and decide if there may be a more sensible approach that could save you money. If you're cooking for others, you'll have to consider their likes and dislikes, and the family's eating patterns. These days many people eat at different times of the day, instead of dining together, and this affects the type of food that is bought.

Next time you go to the supermarket, look at the way other people shop and spend. Those who load their carts with convenience foods, ready-meals, and snacks will be spending far more than others who purchase simple, unprocessed foods. So take a lesson from that and, where possible, stick to the basics. You will find that you'll spend much more money if are buying lots of fashionable snack foods and fillers, so try to resist the temptation, even if you think it's going to save you time.

**Shopping tips**
Before you go shopping, write a list. Check your kitchen stores to make sure that you are not duplicating items that you already have.

If you are feeling really organized, plan the meals for yourself and family for the week to come and buy for those foods. You can buy any extras, such as fresh bread, during the week.

Always go shopping for food alone if you can, and stick to your shopping list. Shopping with others often means that lots of unnecessary and expensive impulse buys end up in your cart— especially if there are children with you!

On certain days of the week, supermarkets cut the price of some of their lines, often just before the end of the day or at the weekend. Time your shopping to take advantage of these useful bargains.

Make the most of products that are reduced because they are close to their sell-by dates. But don't buy foods that you don't need just for the sake of a bargain, and be sure to use them quickly.

Supermarket brands are usually cheaper than manufacturer's branded goods, and some stores have a range of basic foods that are plainly packed and especially good value.

Save money-off vouchers and coupons, but only for items that you really want. There's no value in spending money on things that you don't need.

You could always use a hand-basket instead of a cart in the supermarket – it's one way of restricting your purchases!

Sometimes it's wise to shop locally, where you won't be tempted by the vast array of products on sale in much larger stores.

Get to know your local butcher or fish seller and tell them that you are always on the lookout for a bargain. There's no shame in being a thrifty shopper, so don't be embarrassed about buying ground meat when the customer next to you is buying fillet steak!

Consider buying certain items in bulk – it could work out much cheaper. But avoid falling into the trap of buying foods in bulk and then ending up eating them almost immediately. Sometimes food disappears far too quickly if you have plenty of it.

## Choose cheaper foods

Get to know which foods will really save you money. It may mean choosing some unfamiliar cuts of meat or types of fish, so you might have to catch up on some of your cooking skills, but it will be worth it. Follow the hints and tips here to guide you through some of the ways in which you can choose foods more cheaply.

Choose cheaper cuts of meat. These will need longer, more moist methods of cooking, such as stewing, casseroling, or braising, so that the meat becomes tender and delicious, but you'll find that it's well worth the wait.

Most people invariably go for the straightforward and familiar, particularly when it comes to meat. If you choose something less popular, it's usually cheaper. Short plate of beef, brisket, side of pork, and arm shoulder of pork are all exceptionally good value and very tasty too. Rolled breast of lamb makes a cheap and tasty roast, and neck slices of lamb are superb in stews. Try variety meats too; liver and kidneys are delicious when properly prepared.

Poultry is much cheaper than it used to be, and stores and supermarkets often have offers that are really good value for money. It generally works out much cheaper to buy whole chickens rather than portions, so that you can enjoy the best of the bird, then have the leftovers in a stir-fry or risotto. Make the most of the chicken carcass too, by using it to make stock for soup. If you don't want to make soup immediately, freeze it for later.

If you've never tried baking your own bread, perhaps now is the time to learn. It's a very satisfying thing to do – quite therapeutic! And while there are usually some very good offers for cheap fresh bread in the supermarkets, it's unlikely that they will taste as good as your homemade efforts – what could be fresher than a loaf straight out of the oven.

You can buy all kinds of flours – all-purpose, whole wheat, or mixed grain, for example – to make a variety of interesting breads and rolls. Even specialty breads, such as focaccia, naan breads, etc, which are always the most expensive to buy, are not so difficult to make yourself.

To save on time and fuel, bake a few loaves at once and freeze what you don't need. When they're defrosted, they'll taste as fresh as ever.

## SAVING FUEL

There's not much point in saving lots of money on food if you're going to waste it on fuel. Take account of some of these money saving tips:

Always cover pans to keep in the heat. A heavy cast-iron casserole dish is a good investment, as are some of the heavy-gauge stainless steel ones. They retain heat well, so you can cook over a low heat.

Cooking food in a microwave oven is very cost effective as the food is cooked quickly and efficiently, using very little electricity. An added bonus is that there are generally fewer dishes to do, so you use less hot water.

Make full use of oven space whenever possible. There's not much point in cooking just a couple of baked potatoes when you could make full use of the oven. Plan what dishes you are going to cook, making sure that they will use the same oven temperature.

Avoid opening the oven door when you are cooking. Not only will you be risking the success of your baking, you will be increasing fuel costs.

Cook more than one vegetable at a time by using a steamer stacked on top of a saucepan. This conserves both fuel and the nutritive value of the vegetables.

Even ground beef can be quite highly-priced these days, so make a little go a long way by padding it out with extra vegetables. For instance, if you're making a chili con carne, you can use a little less ground meat and add some more onions, carrots, mushrooms, and red kidney beans to the cooking pot. You won't affect the end result – it will be every bit as tasty, yet considerably cheaper.

A market is often the best and place to buy your fruit and vegetables. You can usually get a far better price per pound than anywhere else, and there are often reductions at the end of the day.

Use fruit and vegetables when they are fresh. That way they will have a higher vitamin content, and they will taste better too. So don't buy too many goods at once, or else your produce will deteriorate before you get the chance to eat it.

Start to use some of the parts of vegetables that you used to throw away. The outer leaves or tougher stalks can all be cooked to make very tasty soups. Once they are chopped finely or puréed, they will taste superb.

If you cut the crusts off sliced bread, make them into breadcrumbs for using in puddings, stuffings, and breadcrumb toppings. Or use them to coat chicken portions or fish. If you don't want to use the breadcrumbs right away, dry them out in a low oven and keep them in an airtight container to use another time.

Canned beans and pulses are great for convenience, but it's much cheaper to soak your own and slow-cook them until tender. Do plenty at the same time, then freeze any that you don't use immediately. Remember, however, that it's important to bring dried red kidney beans to the boil and boil rapidly for 10 minutes, to destroy a harmful toxin in them.

You can easily sprout your own beans for salads and stir-fries – mung beans are usually used. All you need do is wash them, then leave them on paper towels, and keep them well watered until they sprout – this will take 4–5 days. Rinse well before using.

### Freezing foods

A freezer is a good investment for those on a budget. Don't buy one that's larger than you really need, however, as empty freezer space costs money. A full freezer is more efficient, so keep it well stocked up – bread is always a good filler if your stocks are running low.

A freezer means you can buy seasonal produce when it is at its cheapest, make the most of special offers at your supermarket, or freeze any leftovers. If a dish is suitable for freezing, such as a casserole or bake, double the quantities and freeze half – you'll save on fuel and have a ready-made meal just waiting to be reheated whenever you need it. For safety's sake, when reheating frozen foods make sure you heat them thoroughly, to kill any harmful bacteria that may be present.

## Get growing

There are so many books available now on growing your own fruit and vegetables, you may as well start producing your own. Even if you grow only a couple of varieties, you may be able to swap some of them with someone else's homegrown produce to get a good selection. And how good they will taste, freshly picked from your own garden.

If you don't have enough space to grow your own fruit and vegetables, don't give up entirely. You can always grow fresh herbs in a few planters and window boxes. They will make a world of difference to your cooking, and will thrive if you keep cutting and using them.

You don't need much space to plant about three tomato plants – enough to keep you in fresh tomatoes throughout the summer, and give you some for chutney-making too. Green or red bell peppers will do well in containers too, as will zucchini and cucumbers.

Try buying plants or seeds from local gardening clubs, where they are likely to be much cheaper, or swap cuttings with friends and neighbors. You might harvest some friendly advice too.

When it comes to cooking fresh vegetables (whether or not you've grown them yourself) always cook them in a small amount of water for the minimum amount of time. Vegetables should retain their crispness and color – overcooking them only spoils their flavor and reduces their vitamin content.

## Food for free

At certain times of the year, you can take advantage of nature's harvest and help yourself to some free food! Blackberries and a number of other wildsoft fruits are to be enjoyed in September, and they are superb in pies and other desserts as well as for making jelly. Combine them with some apples – the tart flavour complements them perfectly.

Orchards often have an abundant supply of windfalls that you may be allowed to gather. It's a great way to enjoy apples, pears, and plums. Or go gathering nuts if you happen to have nut trees near you.

If your friends offer you their homegrown produce, accept it graciously. They may not want to make a batch of raspberry jelly from their homegrown produce, yet would be glad to see them used by you. The same goes for green tomatoes at the end of the season, which make delicious chutney.

## Keep on cooking

Whatever your reasons are for cooking on a budget, it's very wise to treat food as a precious commodity that deserves careful preparation and treatment. After all, a great deal of time and effort goes into its production. And because waste is so unnecessary and expensive, it makes good sense to eat sensibly and healthily. So do make every effort to enjoy good, honest home-cooked food that doesn't cost a fortune: you'll be doing yourself, and your pocket, a great big favor.

### LEFTOVERS

Don't be tempted to throw away even the smallest amounts of foods or leftovers. It's surprising how they can easily be used to make something tasty.

Leftover vegetables can be used to flavor stocks, soups and stews, or used for omelet fillings or hashes. You can even mash them and form them into little patties, then coat in beaten egg and breadcrumbs, and fry in a little oil.

For your health's sake, treat leftovers with respect – you don't want to end up with a sick family. Always cover and cool cooked leftovers quickly, then refrigerate them. Use them up as soon as possible, and reheat thoroughly where appropriate.

# INDEX

Apples, pancakes with butterscotch sauce and, 68
apricot and banana queen of puddings, 70

Bacon, onion and potato hotpot, 32
baking, 76–7
bananas: apricot and banana queen of puddings, 70
barley: lamb and barley broth, 12
batter: savory batter popovers with thyme and onion sauce, 30
beans, 78
beef: baked stuffed onions, 22
  beef goulash, 18
bread, 77, 78
  chocolate bread pudding, 64
  savory bread and butter bake, 52
butterscotch sauce, pancakes with apples and, 68

Cakes, 76
cheese: cream cheese and fresh herb soup, 8
  golden cheese and leek potato patties, 58
  ground lamb and potato moussaka, 29
  mushroom and Parmesan risotto, 38
  pasta with pine kernels and blue cheese, 41
  savory bread and butter bake, 52
  spinach and cheese pancake stack, 55
  winter vegetable cobbler, 24
chicken: chicken and chili bean pot, 16
  chicken and corn puff, 56
  quick Chinese chicken with noodles, 44
  Thai-style chicken fried rice, 36
chili: chicken and chili bean pot, 16
chocolate bread pudding, 64
choux pastry: chicken and corn puff, 56
cobbler, winter vegetable, 24
cod: mariner's pie, 26
coffee cream trifle, 74
corn: chicken and corn puff, 56
couscous, Moroccan vegetable, 46
cream cheese and fresh herb soup, 8
cucumber dip, 50
curry, egg and garbanzo bean, 50

Desserts, 63–74
dip, cucumber, 50

Eggplant: ground lamb and potato moussaka, 29
eggs: egg and garbanzo bean curry, 50
  flamenco eggs, 60

Fish stew, Italian, 15
flamenco eggs, 60
free food, 79
freezing foods, 78
fruit, 78
fudge sauce, hot, 64
fuel: saving fuel, 78

Garbanzo bean: egg and garbanzo bean curry, 50
golden cheese and leek potato patties, 58
goulash, beef, 18
ground lamb and potato moussaka, 29
growing vegetables, 78–9

Herbs: cream cheese and fresh herb soup, 8
hotpot: bacon, onion, and potato, 32

Italian fish stew, 15

Lamb: ground lamb and potato moussaka, 29
  lamb and barley broth, 12
lasagne, smoked fish, 42
leeks: golden cheese and leek potato patties, 58
  mariner's pie, 26
leftovers, 79
lentil and parsnip potage, 10

Mariner's pie, 26
meat, 77–8
meringue: apricot and banana queen of puddings, 70
Moroccan vegetable couscous, 46
moussaka, ground lamb and potato, 29
mushroom and Parmesan risotto, 38

Noodles, quick Chinese chicken with, 44

Onions: bacon, onion, and potato hotpot, 32
  baked stuffed onions, 22
  savory batter popovers with thyme and onion sauce, 30
ovens, 78

Pancakes: pancakes with apples and butterscotch sauce, 68
  spinach and cheese pancake stack, 55
paprika: beef goulash, 18
parsnips: lentil and parsnip potage, 10
pasta: pasta with pine kernels and blue cheese, 41
  smoked fish lasagne, 42
pearl barley: lamb and barley broth, 12

peppers: beef goulash, 18
pie dough, 76
pine kernels, pasta with blue cheese and, 41
plums: baked semolina pudding with spiced plums, 73
pork: savory batter popovers with thyme and onion sauce, 30
potatoes: bacon, onion, and potato hotpot, 32
  flamenco eggs, 60
  golden cheese and leek potato patties, 58
  ground lamb and potato moussaka, 29
  mariner's pie, 26

Queen of puddings, apricot and banana, 70
quick Chinese chicken with noodles, 44
quick syrup sponge, 66

Red kidney beans: chicken and chili bean pot, 16
rice: mushroom and Parmesan risotto, 38
  Thai-style chicken fried rice, 36
risotto, mushroom and Parmesan, 38

Sauce, hot fudge, 64
saving fuel, 78
savory bread and butter bake, 52
savory batter popovers with thyme and onion sauce, 30
semolina pudding with spiced plums, 73
shopping, 76–7
smoked fish lasagne, 42
soups, 7–12
  cream cheese and fresh herb soup, 8
  lamb and barley broth, 12
  lentil and parsnip potage, 10
spinach and cheese pancake stack, 55
steaming, 78
stews: beef goulash, 18
  chicken and chili bean pot, 16
  Italian fish stew, 15
syrup sponge, quick, 66

Thai fish sauce, 36
Thai red curry paste, 36
Thai-style chicken fried rice, 36
tomatoes: beef goulash, 18
  chicken and chili bean pot, 16
  ground lamb and potato moussaka, 29
trifle, coffee cream, 74

Vegetables, 78

Moroccan vegetable couscous, 46
winter vegetable cobbler, 24

Winter vegetable cobbler, 24

Yogurt: cucumber dip, 50